# Accessing the Kingdom Realms

Del Hungerford

Copyright ©2017 by Del Hungerford

All rights reserved. No part of this publication may be reproduced, stored in a retrieval system or transmitted in any way by any means, electronic, mechanical, photocopy, recording or otherwise, without prior permission of the author except as provided by USA copyright law.

All Scripture is taken from the King James Version (KJV), Public Domain.

Artwork and design by Alice Arlene www.alicearlene.com.

Edited by Lisa Thompson www.writebylisa.com.

ISBN-13: 978-1546860020
ISBN-10: 1546860029

Published by CreateSpace
4900 LaCross Road
North Charleston, SC 29406
USA

I impart to you, dear reader, the freedom to set aside preconceived ideas and experience the kingdom realms through intimacy with YHVH.

# Accessing the Kingdom Realms

# Table of Contents

| | |
|---|---:|
| Introduction | 1 |
| Prelude | 5 |
| Chapter 1: A Wandering Mind | 9 |
| Chapter 2: The Art of Being Childlike | 15 |
| Chapter 3: "The Wedding" | 19 |
| Chapter 4: The Camperdown Elm Tree | 23 |
| Chapter 5: Missed Opportunity? | 29 |
| Chapter 6: The Throne Room | 35 |
| Chapter 7: Car and Flaggers | 41 |
| Chapter 8: Instruments and my Ancestors | 47 |
| Chapter 9: Castle of my Heart | 53 |
| Chapter 10: The Mobile Court | 59 |
| Chapter 11: The Musical Instrument Room | 67 |
| Chapter 12: Orchestration of DNA | 77 |
| Chapter 13: Dividing Soul and Spirit | 83 |
| Postlude | 91 |
| Resources | 95 |
| About the Author | 99 |

# Introduction

These encounters flow from personal experience and daily time spent with the Father. Why do I share them? If what I've walked through can help others find deeper intimacy with the Father, Son, and Holy Spirit, I want to make myself vulnerable to them. However, I only share what can be useful for others. What Papa shows me in my own blueprint for my life is not for public consumption. As you, too, walk through your own encounters in the Kingdom Realms, many of these are meant for your eyes and ears only. Be careful what you share.

You need to walk this out yourself and not take someone else's experience and use that as your framework; <u>you must experience and engage the Kingdom Realms of heaven for yourself</u>. My stories are meant to be a starting point that propels you into intimacy with Father by giving you visuals to help open the eyes of your imagination. I also encourage you to read Scripture to launch you into your journey. Learn to visualize and "step into" what you're reading.

In order to experience what Revelation 4 talks about when John hears a voice beckoning him to "Come up here," you must first realize that this is done through the eyes of your imagination. For some, this might be outside your current paradigm, which will require an adjustment to "see" into the Kingdom Realms.

Throughout this book, I provide several resources to help you on your journey. Since I am sharing my journey, I can only tell you what I have personally experienced. Many of my own experiences came out of practicing what I was reading and listening to. Application and practice is the key, which I'll explain in further detail in the next chapter.

God created us to commune with Him daily. Sure, we can read about Him in the Bible, but spending time in His presence builds relationship. Once I realized this truth, my personal situations began to change. It hasn't been a quick change but one of constant pursuit of God. The key element in all of this: relationship with Father, Jesus, and the Holy Spirit. Out of that relationship flows everything else. <u>Any other approach leads to skewed results.</u>

Developing relationships takes time, so don't expect this journey to be like putting frozen food in a microwave and pressing the thaw button to get to the meat of what Father has for you more quickly. Even if we are the "frozen chosen," the best method of thawing is to allow the natural process to take its course. Forcing the process to happen generally results in additional adverse effects. Do you really want to rush the process just because you desire quicker results? You will need to deal with issues in your life, both past and present. If you view those as opportunities to delve deeper into relationship with Father, you'll be in a better frame of mind to walk through them because Jesus will be at your side to help you.

We've all been hurt and carry trauma in our DNA from our own lives as well as that of our ancestors. As we develop an intimate relationship with YHVH, He helps us clean out the corruption in our DNA. If your earthly father figure is part of existing trauma, begin

## Introduction

the cleansing process there first. Crawl into the lap of YHVH and listen to Him tell you how much you're loved. I suggest that you contact Moed Ministries at www.moed-ministries.com. Click on the "mentoring" tab for further instructions.

Are you ready to begin this journey?

# Prelude

Much of what I learned about how to press into the presence of God came from being a musician. If you've ever studied classical music, you know that it takes many years to become an "artist" performer of any musical instrument. The notes are generally the easy part; they are all about practicing over and over until all the technical passages are cemented into your hands through muscle memory so that your hands consistently function as they should. In comparing that to life habits, we have to practice a new habit or way of thinking in order to cement it into our lifestyle.

For most budding musicians, the most difficult part is learning how to play musically, or in simpler terms, "with feeling." In the Kingdom of God, this compares to developing intimacy with the Father—communing with Him and responding from the heart. When we learn to live out of our spirits instead of our souls, we no longer go through the motions of "doing" Christianity because we're developing intimacy instead. That intimacy then flows through our spirit, into our soul, and then out of our body. Deep intimacy with Father reflects in our behavior, too.

I already know the next question. "How will I find the time for this? I'm so busy!" My response to that question is, "What price are you willing to pay?" And, I don't mean with money. That price might involve paradigm shifts, attitude changes, rearranging your time, and letting go of things you don't need. You might need to dissolve relationships, especially if they are toxic. Of course, the largest cost will come through dealing with soulish and fleshly habits that hold you back: pornography, other sexual issues, addictions, bad attitudes, fear, anger, laziness, apathy, abusive behaviors, and unhealthy thoughts/beliefs we like to "pet" and nurture.

Typical questions I ask people who say there's no time: Do you shower? Do you watch TV? Are you a gamer? Do you cook? Do you clean? Do you drive to work or ride a bus? If you answered "yes" to any of these questions, you have time. It's a matter of changing your thought patterns and, in some cases, behavior patterns. To do that, start by being cognizant of the thoughts, intents, and desires of your heart. Then, practice new thought patterns that shape behavioral patterns. This is called "building character."

We all have choices and those choices, along with our thoughts, words, and intents, frame the personal world in which we live. Even when situations around us are terrible, we can learn how to function from the supply that God has for us. Then, the many horrible events that happen to us, when viewed from the perspective of the Father, take on a whole different meaning. I believe the Scripture "In every thing give thanks: for this is the will of God..." actually means that you're not thanking Him **for** the trials but **in** and **during** trials. (I Thessalonians 5:18 – KJV) It's putting "on a garment of praise for the spirit of heaviness" in life's circumstances to help us through them when we're walking in intimacy with Father (Isaiah 61:3 – KJV).

Next, we look at the fruit in our lives: finances, relationships with people, how you behave around your family and close friends, at work, in public, and so forth. If you don't really know, ask the people closest to you to be honest and then be prepared to not be offended if they say something you disagree with or that's hurtful. Listen with your heart and "hear" what Father is saying through those who really know your behaviors, habits, and attitudes.

If you hear things and then think, "I didn't know I did that," do not allow condemnation, fear, anxiety, accusation, or defensiveness to come and dwell in your heart. Quickly agree with the adversary and repent. By repenting, you remove the enemy's power to dwell in your thoughts, intents, and desires. Do you want to quickly disarm him? Repentance, even if you think you're right, takes care of the accusations against you in the spirit realm. Remember, the Word also says that we wrestle not against flesh and blood but against principalities and other junk in the heavenlies (Ephesians 6). The tough part is walking this out and not allowing accusations to come at you and derail you. We also need to practice "taking every thought captive," according to 2 Corinthians 10:4-5 (KJV). Depending on the situation, you might need to do this several times a day until the soul finally bows to the spirit.

Keep your eyes on the Father. The enemy is only a distraction. When we learn to truly do this, many of those things that continue to nip and bite at our heels have to stop because we quit paying attention to them. When we learn to stop "petting" our sorrows or dwelling on the "would have, could haves, or should haves," we will experience much greater breakthrough. Our focus should be on the Father instead of on the hardships around us. Which will you choose? Is the glass half full or half empty? Do you focus on the negative or positive during tough situations? Look at your first or immediate responses for the answer to these questions.

What I share is from personal experience. Life isn't easy, and very bad things happen to and around us. The outcome is often determined by our attitudes and actions during the worst times in our lives. Had I truly understood this, I might not have gone through so much turmoil after leaving an abusive marriage that nearly cost me my life. Looking back on it now, I can see how that situation brought me into greater intimacy with the Father. In Him, I move, live, and have my being (Acts 17:28 – KJV).

With that, as you read my experiences with Father and Jesus, feel free to use them as a starting point to propel you into intimacy with the Trinity. Practice . . . practice . . . practice!

# Chapter 1

# A Wandering Mind

In my heart garden, under the willow tree, Jesus sits on the bench, waiting. Seeing me, He stands to greet me, enveloping me in a great big bear hug. I feel His love flowing through me, a type of tune-up coming directly from the frequencies flowing from Him.

"Is that what it's like when your healing power flows through people?" I ask, knowing that my physical body is fighting symptoms.

"Yes," Jesus responds. "As you sit in me and allow my frequency, which is light, to soak into you, your body will eventually come into line with its intended function."

"Being 'in You' brings my body into Your frequency, which is Your DNA?" I clarify.

"The more you spend time in My presence, with the Father

and the Holy Spirit, the more your whole being will be changed. Much of that also comes through your thought life. Remember that thoughts, along with the spoken word, create frequency. This is one of the reasons that you must take thoughts captive," He adds. (2 Corinthians 10:5)

I'm silent for a moment as I ponder how thoughts have frequency.

"How do I train my mind not to wander so much when I'm trying to engage?" I ask, while filtering through the many questions bombarding my mind.

Jesus laughs with me as a picture of a wandering thought flits through my mind.

"This is training your mind and cleaning out that gateway. Remember, you've had many years of practice with allowing your mind to do what it wanted. To change that, you must continue to be diligent in cleaning your gateways."

"Much like what I tell my students to do when they are learning something new and correcting bad habits?" I question.

He gazes lovingly into my eyes. I feel the impartation as His eyes pierce through every fiber of my being.

"Yes! You tell them that playing the clarinet is as much mental as it is physically playing the instrument. The Kingdom works the same way. You engage the Kingdom Realms with your imagination, then practice what you learn in the natural. You see first, then do." Jesus explains.

"That makes sense—the more I focus on it, keeping the redemptive side of an issue in my heart, the sooner I'll have victory over it. Is that right?" I clarify.

I look up at the canopy of the giant willow tree covering us while letting Jesus' words sink into my heart. The leaves and branches sway to the worship coming from the throne.

"When you hold onto My Word, keeping it in your heart, you begin to change as you line that up with action. Many people see and hear My words but then do nothing about them. As you also say, you need some perseverance of consistency for breakthrough. Many quit too early and then wonder why situations in their lives don't change."

Processing through this in my imagination, I see the mind gate as a doorway, opening and closing, allowing only those things coming from my spirit to enter into the gate. I giggle to myself as I watch the door close to junk trying to come from my soul.

"If I'm hearing You correctly, I need to keep the issue of a wandering mind before me and be very diligent to not allow my mind to do what it wants. My spirit gateways control my mind gate . . . ."

"And, when your soul finally bows down to the spirit, you will have the division of soul and spirit." He finishes my sentence, looking me in the eyes.

I understand through more than just His words as He pulls me closer, where once again, I feel His vibrations from within flow into me.

**The Lesson in This**

When I first started this journey of learning to function in the Kingdom Realms, I had so many questions! I learned the best way to find answers was to go directly to the Father, Jesus, and the Holy Spirit. Yes, I listened to a **lot** of teachings, but often, those teachings brought more questions. Even so, the teachings were great catalysts that helped me engage on my own.

I'd sometimes listen to another's encounter over and over,

form a picture in my mind of what that might look like, and use it as a springboard for my own journey into intimacy. It took some time before I could see much because I had to exercise my imagination, which had become dulled by the cares of this world.

I had just started learning that we have gateways in our body, soul, and spirit before this encounter. We must learn how to function out of our spirit, not the soul. My questions here focused on how my mind tends to wander no matter what I do. My mind had an opening, permitting access via the soul gateways that required some attention, which meant that I had to focus on cleaning out this area.

You will notice as you read this book that I'm shown dark places in my life. I had to clean them out, bringing light and life into them. You will experience the same thing if your goal is to develop intimacy. We have to be willing to take our "junk to the dump" as we go into further intimacy with Father. If not, we won't be able to handle His glory. We'll essentially be at a place of standstill until we're willing to clean out those dark places: what we fear, the words and actions of others that have hurt us, our "stinking thinking," and so forth.

**Chapter Resources**
- Mike Parson's videos on YouTube are grouped according to subject under his playlists. Check for "gateways of our spirit, soul, body."
- Ian Clayton has a book titled <u>Gateways of the Three-fold Nature of Man</u> available on his website and through Amazon. His teaching, "I Can See," helps you understand seeing in the spirit.

- **Terms:**
  - o Gateways: A place of authority and dominion where we control what goes in and out. We have three sets of gateways: spirit, soul, and body. The mind gate is one of the soul gateways.
  - o Dividing the soul and spirit: This is scriptural reference from Hebrews 4:12 (KJV) "For the word of God is quick, and powerful, and sharper than any two-edged sword, piercing even to the dividing asunder of soul and spirit, and of the joints and marrow, and is a discerner of the thoughts and intents of the heart."

# Chapter 2

# THE ART OF BEING CHILDLIKE

"The Wedding" plays . . . Jesus and I dance to the rhythm of the music under the willow tree. He leads me in this waltz as we move around effortlessly under the tree together. As the song ends, we walk through a clearing and into the open. Animals greet us as we start to follow a cobblestone path through the middle of a well-manicured field of grass. Nothing else is in sight as I focus on the glittery path.

Together, we skip like children playing hopscotch. We giggle and laugh at the sheer joy of being together. I'm seeing Jesus in a playful, childlike mode, which encourages the same behavior from me. I can tell this makes Him happy because He knows that I like to be silly and have fun.

"That's right!" He chimes in as He skips in front of me. "What's in you was put there by me. There's nothing to be ashamed of so . . . be you!"

He sticks out His tongue and immediately runs further down the path.

"Wait for me!" I yell while running after Him.

A deer runs in front of me and catches up to Jesus. They gaze at each as Jesus stops for a moment. I can see the love and glory flowing from Jesus to the deer. The deer seems to rely on this "fuel" to keep it going. As I catch up, the deer runs off. Jesus turns His attention back to me, and we take off again down the path.

I ponder my time with Jesus as we come to a stop further up the cobblestone path after He beat me there by quite a bit. For many years, I didn't allow myself to be childlike because my paradigm told me that I had to grow up and stop being silly. This interaction with Jesus brings me freedom and permission to act goofy and be silly.

"Certain attitudes, character, and thoughts must be well established in you in order to move where I'm calling you." Jesus says, responding to my thoughts.

As we stand at the edge of the path, looking off into the distance, I stare as far as my eyes can see. A golden sun is setting behind a mountain range. Somehow, I sense this is a reflection of an end to one season and a beginning to another. It's a matter of walking up to and into the other side. The "play" won't stop, but it will change. I feel the importance of learning to be free.

"Your destiny scroll looks like no one else's. You can't compare yourself to what others are supposed to do. For you, the child-like freedom is part of what's in your DNA, which is part of your scroll. When you feel a heaviness come at you due to others' expectations of you, remember to stay in a place of rest to be who you are. Don't let others frame your world by allowing negative, critical, or derogatory comments to enter that place of rest," Jesus instructs.

"So, my playfulness—even though it can annoy people—is part of me?" I ask.

"You are unique like everyone else is unique. Playfulness and silliness is part of you. There are those . . . ."

"Like Todd?" I think.

"There are those, like your ex-husband Todd, whom have been an intimate part of your life that encouraged you to change to their paradigm of how a grown-up should act. Your silly songs in the espresso business released a frequency of joy and playfulness that many people wanted to be around. Do you wonder why the business failed once you sold it? The joy was gone. Attitudes carry frequency. When you align your frequency with mine, this releases joy into the atmosphere around you. Those who don't like it are the ones who feed off the negative. It's all they know. Changing a paradigm takes practice, perseverance, and patience," Jesus smiles.

I look into His eyes at the small mischievous twinkle. He pulls me close as we watch the sun set on one season, awaiting the sunrise of a new one.

## The Lesson in This

What is growing up really all about? Why is it that we have to act according to the dictates of society? Yes, I understand that some actions are inappropriate at certain times, but to generally shut someone down for being silly is a form of control. Jesus knew what I'd gone through in my marriage, and this encounter was His way of helping me understand that my childlike fun was acceptable to Him.

Being in this place with Him gave me some freedom in an area that I had previously tried to keep at bay because I thought something was wrong with me.

Many of us struggle with our identity. This encounter was about understanding part of my identity and how aspects of my personality help me be who I was meant to be. When we learn to function from who we are in Christ, our lives flow much more smoothly.

Jesus knows each of us much better than we know ourselves. How He appears to me won't necessarily be the same way He appears to you. This is like an inside joke when only two of you know the meaning. Jesus will speak to you in language that you can understand. He often speaks to me in musical language because I can relate to it. He cracks little jokes that only I understand, and as we spend time together, we create special moments that are meant for just the two of us. It will be the same for you, too.

**Chapter Resources**
- Ian Clayton has two teachings on his website titled "The Testimony of Your Scroll" and "Strengthening Your Spirit."
- Mike Parsons has a teaching set, "The Transformation Series," that is part of the "Engaging God" series and can be found on this website.
- Terms:
    - Destiny or testimony scroll: the mandate/blueprint for your life that as a spirit being, you agreed to with YHVH in the beginning. See Jeremiah 1:5.

# Chapter 3

# "The Wedding"

    I sit quietly beside the river of life, watching the fish play around almost as if they're putting on a colorful show for me. A breeze comes up, and I hear leaves rustling in the trees behind me. Turning, I notice the branches and leaves of the willow tree swaying to a rhythm. Curious, I rise and saunter over to the bench under the willow tree. After sitting down, I stare up into the tree canopy and watch the branches and leaves move in time to the rhythm of something . . . .

    Not quite sure what to think of this movement, my mind is drawn back to my home. I then realize the music for "The Wedding" is playing, and the willow tree, in the Kingdom Realms, appears to be reacting to the music in my house.

From my right, I hear a chuckle.

"Everything is connected between the earth and the Kingdom Realms, so it would only make sense that what's up here would respond to what you do on the earth," Papa says, joining me on the bench.

We both watch the entire tree react to the music playing in my living room, swaying perfectly in rhythm to the waltz. Without further words, Papa takes me in His arms, and we begin to dance to the music. I follow His strong lead. He seems to know when my steps aren't as steady as His, so He waits until I become more in sync with His motions. We twirl around, matching our movements and rhythm with the branches in the tree.

I look down and notice Papa is wearing a tuxedo with black shiny shoes. His hair, the color of gold strands, is woven into perfection. His face illuminates in glory. As He moves, waves of light shoot out from Him into the surrounding atmosphere. They, too, move to the rhythm of the music.

I then notice what I'm wearing: a beaded gown, much like Cinderella's. I can't really tell what color it is since it's full of gems that sparkle with every color. My hair cascades over my shoulders and down my back, and it, too, glistens like glitter.

Together, we dance. I sense this dance is about me learning to follow His lead. At the thought, Papa smiles.

I gaze deeply into His eyes. As on previous occasions, I see what I can only explain as everything – earth, sky, creation, the present, the future, and scene after scene of some movie. There's so much to see that I don't know how to choose what to see first. I sense that the most important thing to do right now is to learn how to dance as I'm following His lead with ease and that these movies will be viewed in due time.

"Wisdom has spoken to you." He quietly responds. "Yes, it's important to watch and learn so that you can take My lead. It's like a dance. As you learn to look like Me and walk with Me, Jesus, and the Holy Spirit, what you see will then come into greater focus."

Although I can still see the movie playing, I look once again into His eyes and focus on following His movements. It's not like a normal waltz but more like one where the movements can change. I realize that when I keep my focus on His eyes, my feet seem to know what to do. My whole being responds to the love in His eyes.

We dance the night away . . . .

**The Lesson in This**

During this encounter, I learned where to keep my eyes. Since everything in the supernatural is mirrored in the natural, I learned to keep my eyes on the Father. As long as I did that, my steps were ordered.

He also gave me insight about looking into the Father's eyes and seeing everything flash before me. When you're "in Him," you have the capability to see all that He has for you. I understood that my part of this waltz was to learn to "live, and move, and have our being" in him (Acts 17:28 – KJV).

In the beginning, I have music playing in my home; music I created while listening to what was coming up through my spirit. Therefore, it seems natural that everything in the Kingdom Realms reacts to what I'd created. Until this encounter, I hadn't really thought about that. It encourages me to know that all of heaven enjoys interacting with my creative abilities. It will be the same with you. When the Father has given you creative ideas or shown you strategies on how to do something, all of heaven rejoices with you as you fulfill what's on your life's blueprint or scroll of testimony. My encouragement here is to not simply throw away those thoughts that seem to come from left field that waft through your mind even if you wonder, "Where did that come from?" Maybe the Father is in those fleeting thoughts, and it really wasn't the pizza you ate last night. The only way to know is to ask Him and see what He says.

**Chapter Practice and Resources**
- Ian Clayton has a series titled "The Spirit of Wisdom" along with another teaching, "The Seven Spirits of God," that introduces all the seven spirits and what they do.
- Mike Parson's series of teachings on the subject are titled "7 Spirits" and are found on his YouTube playlist.
- Grant and Samantha Mahoney have a teaching set titled "Quantum Entanglement with the Government of God," which goes into great depth for each of the seven spirits of God.

## Chapter 4

# THE CAMPERDOWN ELM TREE

Sitting by the river of life, I ponder my night of dancing with Papa and the subsequent days in the garden of my heart. In this place, I have a beautiful field of wild flowers, my bench by the river, and another bench under my willow tree.

Here, I'm at peace. I also just learned that I can actually plant things in my garden! I'm excited as I wonder what to plant!

"How about that Camperdown elm tree?" says a voice from behind me.

"I love my Camperdown elm! Can I plant one here, too?" I ask, looking around to see where the voice is coming from.

"Yes!" I hear as I see a figure come into focus.

Is it Jesus or Papa? I think as I squint my eyes, searching . . . .

Hearing my thoughts, the voice says, "As you spend time with us, you'll know the difference between us simply by the sound our voice."

I can see but not clearly at the moment. Continuing to stare toward the sound of the voice, I know it's either Jesus or Papa. Then, I see a bearded face materialize right before me. The rest of a body shape appears, but only the face is visible. I can tell its Jesus by His eyes.

"Tricked you, didn't I?" He jokes.

As I continue to look into His eyes, His whole being comes into focus.

"Well, that was quite odd to suddenly see your face right in front of me." I say, laughing.

I can tell Jesus wants to have a bit of fun with me since His grin looks much like the Cheshire cat. The thought of this makes me giggle.

"So, are you going to plant that elm tree?" He asks.

"Where do I find it?" I ask, looking around to see if there might happen to be a tree somewhere near that I can plant.

"Speak it into existence," He answers.

"What do you mean?" I say in a confused tone, continuing to look around.

"Say its name. Call it into existence."

Thinking about this for a moment, I also realize that I need to decide where to plant the tree. I see the bench by the river has no trees near it. Maybe this is why this all seems treeless because I have yet to plant any.

"You cultivate this garden like you do an earthly garden," He replies, answering my thoughts.

"That makes sense. I'd never thought of that before."

Still pondering Jesus' words about speaking the tree into

# The Camperdown Elm Tree

existence, I go to the bench and look around. I want the tree to provide a canopy over the bench, so I stand behind it right where I want the tree planted. Not quite knowing what to do next, I mull over what to say.

"Just speak it forth," Jesus answers as He walks over next to me.

"Camperdown elm, be planted in this spot," I command authoritatively.

After I speak forth the words, I bend over and dig a hole as a prophetic act so that I can place a seed that I don't yet have in the ground. The moment that I start digging, a trowel appears in my left hand, and a seed appears in my right hand. After preparing the spot, I place the seed into the ground and cover it up. Seeing the river of life running by, I know that I need to water the spot. How do I get heavenly water? The river of life isn't an actual liquid so, I try to wrap my brain around how to channel water that isn't really water from the river of life to the tree.

Giggling, Jesus asks, "How did you get the seed?"

"I spoke to it."

"Then, speak to the river and tell it to go water the seed."

Without further questions, I say loudly, "River of life, go water my seed."

A cloud-like mist rises from the river past me and hovers over the area where I planted the seed. As I watch, the seed begins to sprout. I feel as if I'm watching a time-lapsed video. The mist stays in and around the tree, constantly "watering" it. Although it's not really water, I can tell it's providing some type of nourishment because the tree soaks up every bit of mist. When that's gone, more mist appears.

"This is much like what you experience on earth. As you remember, what you plant there takes time to grow. What you're planting here will also take time to be seen on earth. Remember that everything you do here will be manifest on earth in due season," Jesus informs me.

"I know that I want the Camperdown elm, but I don't necessarily know why," I ponder.

"What do Camperdown elms do?" He asks.

"They provide a canopy or a covering over a certain area, much like those huge ones up on the University of Idaho campus by Ridenbaugh Hall that are growing over the entire sidewalk," I say, picturing what we used to call umbrella trees that cover the sidewalk in front of Ridenbaugh in my mind.

"Exactly! When you plant this tree, you're providing a covering over an area where you rest, on this bench, much like what you'll be doing in the natural when you move to your new place. It will be a place of rest for those who need it," Jesus says excitedly.

"I get it! Planting this tree is then setting into motion that same type of covering on earth—my new home."

"Yes, and as you cultivate it here, the 'tree' will grow there, too," Jesus exclaims as He realizes I'm grasping the concept.

"Wow! All the more reason for me to take my Camperdown elm tree to the new property when I move," I respond with greater insight.

"Again, this is a point of engagement for entering into My presence. You've heard others call it a trigger or anchor point. In a sense, you learn to use what's in the natural to propel you into intimacy with Father, myself, and the Holy Spirit. When you look out your back door every day and see that tree now, you'll have a natural image in front of you as a point of engagement with the tree in your heart garden."

"Thank you so much for that revelation!" I say, giving Jesus a big bear hug.

We then sit on my bench, the Camperdown elm now beginning to provide a covering there. I'm amazed at the alarming rate at which it's growing!

We sit quietly while I lay my head on Jesus' breast where I know I'm in a place of rest.

**The Lesson in This**

As in the previous encounters, Jesus uses examples that are near and dear to me, in this case, my love for Camperdown elm trees. These special hybrid trees cover the sidewalks leading from Ridenbaugh Hall, the music practice building, all the way up to the administration building on the University of Idaho campus. Since I almost majored in forestry, I was drawn to unique-looking trees and plants. When I first saw the Camperdown elm tree, I fell in love with how it cascades downward like an umbrella rather than growing straight up like most trees. In my current home, I have one of these magnificent trees as a focal point in my yard.

Once again, I gained understanding in how "planting" works. As we cultivate what's planted in our hearts, we see the effects of that in our personal lives. The Word says that out of the abundance of the heart, the mouth speaks (Matthew 12:34). This was my opportunity to take and plant something that represented a type of covering in my heart. Further revelation will eventually determine how that will look in the natural.

I believe that each item we plant in our heart garden represents something we are to plant in the natural. In this case, what's in my heart is covered and protected with the love of Jesus. Notice at the end, I sit with Him under the tree in my place of rest.

This can then become a new trigger/anchor point for me when I look into my backyard every morning and see the beautiful Camperdown elm growing by my back fence.

## Chapter Practice and Resources

- Ian Clayton's teachings "God's Garden My Garden" and "The Four Chambers of the Heart."
- One of the first places I visited with Jesus was in my heart garden. I didn't know what it was at the time, but after hearing some teachings on it, I finally understood a bit more about this concept. Ascend into the Kingdom Realms and imagine yourself sitting in your heart garden. What does it look like? Write down what you see. Then, imagine Jesus with you in that place. Have a conversation with Him. Be sure to write down everything. That way, you can go back and start right where you left off, even if it's a month or so later. Each time you go back, write down more of what you see. Add to the experience!
- Terms:
    - Heart garden: An intimate place deep inside you that's meant for communion with YHVH. In the spirit realm, it's seen as a garden where we are to plant and cultivate it.

## Chapter 5

# MISSED OPPORTUNITY?

"Jesus, I want to accomplish what I need to and still feel like I can do what's on my testimony scroll. This whole idea of learning how to function out of the Kingdom Realm while living here on earth is an interesting concept," I ponder while ascending.

I hear Jesus laugh at my thoughts as He greets me. Then, from seemingly out of nowhere, we are standing on a path together. I'm not sure where we are because I can see nothing for what appears to be miles. He looks around in response to my thoughts.

"This is a slate yet to be written," Jesus says while motioning to the vast expanse of nothingness. I see a path in the middle of flat green fields. It's not ugly, but you can tell that when it grows, it's going to be spectacular.

"This is much like what you're experiencing right now. You have a taste of what's there for you, so much more awaits you, just like this field will become much more." He adds as we both look across the field.

I blink, and the field transforms into a field of flowers with a beautiful mountainous region as a backdrop. Every variety of flowers has sprung to life as far as the eye can see. We both gaze at the sudden change.

"This is how fast things can change—in the blink of an eye! Don't be too concerned with where you aren't but watch where you'll be as you spend more time learning how to function in your testimony scroll. As you continue to bask in our presence and watch what we do and how we do it, you, too, will learn," Jesus instructs.

"I think my problem is that, sometimes, I feel like I'm so far behind because of all the years I've missed," I say sadly.

"Yes, you have missed opportunities. However, you have not missed other open doors. Learn from the ones you did miss so that the most important ones, which are yet to come, you won't miss," He offers with a stern yet loving look.

We both turn our gaze at the field again. I notice that streams and even rivers are flowing through it. By now, I can hear a waterfall off in the distance. Birds sing in a chorus that I know is worship.

"Most everyone has missed opportunities because they've believed lies from the enemy. Those lies often come through people who love them very much that have also listened to lies and embraced them. They decided those lies were more real than the truth. They base this on what they see that frames their world. Then, that becomes creative power to transform thoughts into words and then acted upon so that words become a reality."

"I think I'm beginning to understand. That's why words are so

Missed Opportunity?

important. Well, thoughts, too. Everything starts there. I've actually seen thought 'sound' waves up here in the throne room and other places, too. I assume that's how you can hear and respond to thoughts in heaven?" I ask.

"Yes! As you've researched and even seen, thoughts do create frequency. In the human body, thoughts very much affect your physical nature, which is why people often end up so sick. Thoughts literally frame your world. That's why it's so important to divide the thoughts from intents so that seeds of intent don't grow when unsanctified thoughts try to take root . . . ." Stopping for a moment in mid-sentence, He looks at me, studying me.

"Look at the field again," He encourages, pointing towards the mountain. "This was all created because of the creative authority by the sons of God when sanctified thoughts become sanctified intents. The seed bed is then in its purest form to grow amazing and mature desires. However, it all comes out of your position in knowing who you are in the Kingdom Realms. You were meant to create. As you continue to walk in my desires for you, your desires come out of my desires and create reality, much like you are seeing here."

For a moment, I think back to when I was breathing on the stars.

"That was similar," Jesus answers. "What's different with what you did there and what you're seeing here is this is creating something new from nothing. When you breathed on the stars, you were taking what had become corrupted through the fall and breathing new life upon it. The process for each of these is very different."

"I understand now."

"And, as you grow in authority, what you learn and do up here will have more of a positive effect on earth. The opposite is true, too. When you do things out of immaturity, those who are more mature will come to clean up your messes, just as parents clean up small children's messes. I know that I keep repeating this, but, as you move into your authority, out of maturity, you establish a new position that then enables you to move into what you've been called to do as a son. Many years of chaos are waiting for restoration."

I know this is true. As we sit in silence, looking over this field that has now grown into a beautiful meadow teeming with life, I ponder all that Jesus has said. We stand close, holding hands. In this place, I feel love literally flowing from Him into me. I don't wish to leave here any time soon.

**The Lesson in This**

We all feel that we've missed opportunities. We do something stupid and then spend a long time beating ourselves up over the mistake. We dwell on the mistake, afraid of making another, so we simply quit. Honestly, where will that get us?

In these situations, it's too easy to make no decision because we're fearful of what will happen if we make the wrong choice. However, not making a decision is still making a decision. This is about fear and what it does to us. If we don't make mistakes, we don't learn. We live in a society that frowns upon mistakes. However, I've learned the most from some of my stupidest mistakes. Now that I'm past them, I can laugh at myself. What did I learn? Important lessons on what to do, what not to do, and how to see what the Father says about my choices and decisions.

My personal opinion is that we miss opportunities because we're afraid. We might fear anything from the fear of failure to the fear of success. Fear is straight from the pit of hell. The worst part is that once we start to walk in fear, the accuser has won. I don't know about you, but that bugs me! Fear is simply another "food" that helps the enemy gorge himself, making him happy and fat.

As I said previously, much of this is about our identity in Christ. When we know who we are and the authority we carry, we can walk in that authority. Decisions about everything in life become much easier. No fear is associated with making decisions. When we do mess up, which will probably still happen, we won't engage in negative self-talk. You know what I mean. "You dummy! How could you do that?" "Why can't I be smarter than that?" "What will others think?"

In the long run, what matters most is our intimacy with YHVH. Out of that intimacy comes the understanding of who we are. Then, when we make mistakes, we won't let the usual comments come flying out of our mouths. The Scripture that I referenced earlier, "out of the abundance of the heart, the mouth speaks," applies here. The first words that come flying out of our mouths when we've done something stupid help us determine what's in our hearts.

As we begin to walk in who we are in Christ, the negative thoughts, words, and actions that have framed our world begin to fall by the wayside. We become an image of Jesus because we are replacing what's in us with what's in Him. This takes time, perseverance, and practice.

## Chapter Resources

- Ian Clayton has several teachings on creation. Search them and listen to anything about Adam, how he was created, how we fit into that, and anything that involves how things were in the beginning.
- Dr. Adonijah Ogbonnaya (Dr. O) has a teaching set on the Moed Ministries website titled "Convergence Intensive."
- Grant and Sam Mahoney's teaching is available as a conference set on the Moed Ministry website and is titled "Taste and See."

# Chapter 6

# THE THRONE ROOM

I stand, looking at the throne as colors move around the room where they dance to the beat and motion of movements of those present. Angels, other beings that I don't recognize, those in the cloud of witnesses, and other people are present. It's almost as if we're conducting the colors as a group, all in unison. We move, and the colors follow suit. Wide-eyed, I watch in amazement at this "symphony" of sound and movement.

I now have a sense of what it's like to be in the presence of my Beloved, twenty-four hour worship around the throne with all of heaven responding. Flags, dancers, and the whole of heaven moves into and through worship if that's even possible. I see it but can't explain it; it's perfect unity.

After what seems like a long time, I find myself back under my willow tree where I've met with Jesus many times. I know this place to be in the garden of my heart—a very intimate place with my Beloved.

Sitting on the bench alone, I ponder the many places in heaven that I want to learn more about. However, I understand that first of all, I must continue to build relationship with YHVH, my Father as well as my friend.

"As you continue to seek me and spend time in my presence, more will be revealed to you," Jesus says as He comes to join me on the bench.

"I understand. At times, it would be nice if it actually felt more real than it does," I offer in a frustrated tone.

"You must learn to walk in faith. Remember Zechariah 4:6: It's not by might but by my spirit. As you walk that out, you'll be given more responsibility. That responsibility comes to a position, as you've heard taught," He responds while looking at me with love emanating from His eyes.

"You know, I'm not sure that I fully understand what that means . . . out of position?" I ask, looking at Him directly in the eyes.

"You will in time. Sitting on your mountain and then your kingly throne have both been a start. You will gain an understanding that comes with walking in that position as you learn to carry an authority so that you can rule from that position. This will come from watching and learning."

"I get that, but where am I to be watching and learning?"

I'm confused and am not even sure that I know what to ask or how to ask it. I see with my imagination, but I doubt what I see at times and wonder if it will ever be like seeing through my natural eyes.

# The Throne Room

"You come up here like you have been. Notice that you started out in the throne room tonight worshiping. You observed many things moving in unison and all of heaven responding to that movement. I've taken you many other places to show you an overview of what I'm doing to prepare you for maturity. You have so much more to learn in a short amount of time. You must continue to come up here so that you learn all that I have for you in the appointed time. Pay attention to what you see when you visit. Ask questions and learn from your observations. You of all people understand how and what to practice because of your classical music training. Keep that in mind as you continue this walk and engage in the Kingdom Realms so that you can learn about and then practice your responsibility. As with all things, you need to engage in observation time before 'doing' time."

Jesus looks into me, and I feel His eyes pierce deep inside me. This piercing helps me understand and feel what He's saying. Closing my eyes, I continue to ponder spending time with my Beloved. As I do this, I'm back in the throne room again, right where I left off.

Flags of all colors move back and forth from right to left and then from left to right. As they wave, colors and sparkles shoot from them like fireworks into even higher realms. I see some angels respond to the movement of the flags by grabbing the exploding colors and dancing with them. I know that I'm seeing frequencies that shouldn't be tangible but are in this place. Everything intermingles and responds to movement, sounds, and worship.

I turn to the right as I glimpse someone doing cartwheels in front of the throne, followed by a line of others doing cartwheels. As they flip, colors and sparks fly off their hands and feet in all directions. These interact with lightning and thunder coming from the throne. While the explanation sounds chaotic, the actions all fit together, each having its own part in this worship.

I know deep within my core that the more time I spend here, the more I'll understand worship in heaven. With abandonment, I join in.

## The Lesson in This

This experience was one of the first I'd had in the throne room. By this time in my understanding of "coming up here" into the Kingdom Realms, I was beginning to see more in my imagination. However, I was frustrated because others saw more than I did, and I still wanted more. What I had to learn is that this growth all comes with time and practice. Jesus, in His most awesome gentle manner, helped me understand that it's by faith that I continue to practice and learn.

The throne room is an amazing place where everything moves, lives, and functions as one unit. Over the course of several months, I continued to come back to this place, gaining more understanding into what I saw each time. Basically, I built upon previous experiences for a deeper understanding.

The main lesson in this experience is to keep going, asking for more, each time you engage. If you don't understand, ask questions. I find that when I grab my journal and write what I see, I have no time to second guess what I'm writing. I simply write and try to keep up. Then, when I go back later and reread what I've written, I'm amazed! I often don't recognize what I've written, which is good. This takes me out of myself and allows what I'm seeing to take front and center stage.

I recommend that you do the same—as Jesus, Father, and Holy Spirit take you places in the Kingdom Realms, grab a journal and write down what you see. The key to all of this is to not censor yourself and to write freely. If you don't, you won't be able to keep track of the various experiences, making it difficult to go back and reengage. Like with anything in life, you build precept upon precept. In order to effectively do that, you need to have a record of what you previously did.

## Chapter Practice and Resources

- Ian Clayton has a wonderful teaching titled "Intimacy" along with a teaching set "This is Who I Am."
- I can't stress enough how important journaling is during this process. For those of you who've done very little of it, consider this an opportunity to shift some paradigms in your life. For those who can't type and who hate to write, you can use programs, such as Dragon Speech Recognition Software or the Speech to Text app in Google Docs, which will allow you to dictate your thoughts.
- Practice, practice, and when you're done, practice some more.
- Terms:
    - Mountains: Mountains in the spiritual realm are areas of authority. Our personal mountain is a place where we rule and judge from our spirits, in Christ.

## Chapter 7

# CAR AND FLAGGERS

I see a car that looks like a bat mobile from the Batman comics fly above a group of beings worshiping with flags. I chuckle as I think of a scene from Back to the Future where the cars are all flying. But this scene is much more colorful, and the car moves with the motions of those flagging. When they move the flags one way, the car also flies in that same direction, literally dancing in the atmosphere. I immediately sense that the car represents a ministry as often described in dream interpretation. I watch this scene for a bit before I realize that Jesus is standing next to me.

"You can see how important motion is," He pipes up while following the movements of those flagging. "Notice how those flagging all move in similar ways but aren't focused on what the others are doing?"

"Yes, I was observing that," I answer.

"They are responding to a flow and frequency of the direction for that ministry, represented in the car. They move in unison because they're caught up in the same frequency. They are literally tuned into the chord of frequencies that make up a whole. Watch a bit longer," He instructs while pointing to the car.

As we continue to watch, I see opposite motions that flow together, representing the seven colors of the rainbow. I know people are waving the flags, but all I see are the flags. They move harmoniously, a perfectly orchestrated and choreographed "dance" of flags.

"You're right. It's all harmonious, like a musical chord, perfectly tuned. You can see that by how these flags move; the car is affected simply by their motions," Jesus adds.

"I see the movement, but the car seems to be going back and forth. Why is it not moving forward very much?" I ask, puzzled.

"Ah!" Jesus exclaims. "It's like everything else—a learning process. In order for forward motion to occur, a type of rocking back and forth to gain momentum often happens first. This rocking is sometimes seen as failures or setbacks. Those flagging represent flowing out of your spirit, which then sets the direction of the ministry or call written in a testimony scroll. The key is to know what's in that scroll so that you can have more forward motion as you learn to walk in my ways."

I look back at the flaggers and see that they are in full worship. The car drives in circles, then suddenly shoots straight forward at breakneck speed.

"You just witnessed what happens when the momentum reaches a launching point. The circles and rocking back and forth also begin a preparation that's launched by worship and spending time with us in our presence."

I watch in amazement as the car speeds off so quickly that within seconds, it disappears altogether, obviously heading to a new place.

"So, what you're saying is that even though things might appear as if they are at a standstill or even moving backwards at times, that's part of the process of launching?" I ask.

"What you witnessed is an example of how faith works even through trials that appear to cause setbacks. Did you notice that the car was facing the same direction the whole time?"

"Yes. I wondered about that."

"As you mature, you're able to continue looking forward, no matter the circumstance, so that when the launching happens, you're facing the right direction."

Once again, I look at where the car first appeared. The flags still move in harmony almost as if waiting for the next car to arrive. More questions float through my mind, almost too many to even think about, as I continue to watch those flagging.

"How do I begin to learn and understand more about the person of YHVH?" I ask, after pondering numerous questions.

"Keep on doing what you are doing and be expectant. Remember: vision, visitation, and then, habitation. Focus on building that relationship, and it will happen. Practice, my dear . . . practice!" Jesus says, smiling.

## The Lesson in This

In this experience, the visual lesson helped me to understand that the Kingdom Realms work by faith. As I watched the car move back and forth, in my natural mind, I thought, "Why doesn't it go somewhere? What's wrong?" I didn't ask, "What's right?" That was my first mistake.

Look again closely at what Jesus says to me. The motion of moving back and forth represents the actual direction of the car. The key is the direction the car's facing—forward! When we turn around, putting our backs to what YHVH has for us, it's as if we're losing faith. In this image, keeping the car facing forward is similar to what Paul talks about when you keep running ahead towards the prize in Philippians 3:14. As long as we're looking forward in faith, we seem to be in position for the launch when it happens. Much of that comes out of being prepared even through trials along with YHVH's timing for the launch. However, if we're not facing forward, we can easily miss the launch.

The lesson that I gather from this experience is to keep my eyes on Father. As I seek direction, I'm in the proper position to move forward when it's time. We can keep our eyes on the prize, and even in circumstances that don't make sense, we are still in position for that launching point. This even applies when our circumstances seem to be moving backwards.

In situations where others make stupid choices, we can take care of the "spiritual wickedness in high places" (Ephesians 6:12) through the courts of heaven. This is not dealing with people but with the principalities that are in control. I speak more on the courts later in the book.

## Chapter Practice

- As Father shows you subjects that don't appear to make sense, be sure to ask Him for understanding. This experience was all about helping me understand that what I thought were setbacks in my life were more than likely opportunities to learn. The key here is to keep your eyes ahead in the midst of circumstances that can pull you into a slump. Even in those hard places, your eyes can still remain on the Father. Practice keeping your focus during situations that are tough. Use Scripture as an anchor point. One of my favorite verses as a child was ". . . all things work together for good to them that love God, to them who are the called according to his purpose (Romans 8:28). I had that one plastered all over my room and relied on it to carry me through many tough times. Find Scriptures that anchor and ground you in times of difficulty.

## Chapter 8

# INSTRUMENTS AND MY ANCESTORS

Standing outside the throne room, I hear worship and can see it resonating through all of heaven as well as going through me. I begin to dance and twirl and do so for quite some time before I notice that Wisdom is standing next to me.

Without saying anything, we clasp hands and dance to the music, our motions in perfect unison with the sounds. We don't need to learn the steps or ask what the other is doing; we seem to know intuitively what to do. I follow Wisdom's lead, our long, layered robes flowing to the music.

The next thing I know, I have flags and begin to wave them. They change colors, depending on the different movements. Waving them side to side above my head, they turn orange. When I wave them lower, they become deep blue. When I wave them out to the sides in an up-and-down motion, they turn a beautiful bright green. I'm not sure how this happens, but I'm still dancing with Wisdom while waving flags at the same time. Although I'm a bit confused as to how this is possible, I continue. I then remember that everything in heaven responds to worship coming directly from the throne.

Wisdom acknowledges my thoughts before saying, "Come with me. I have more to show you."

The flags seem to disappear, and we're off to another place. Almost as quickly as I can blink, we're on a cobblestone path, walking hand-in-hand.

"We're here now," She says, pointing toward an ornate cobblestone doorway.

I gaze at the door in curiosity, noticing that it also appears to be made of stone. I stand, staring at the door.

"Well, are you going in?" Wisdom asks.

"I wasn't sure that I was supposed to yet," I respond.

"You will eventually go ahead and step forward as you learn that you don't always have to second-guess the voice within you. Trust that when you ask for answers and direction, you will receive them although they might not come in the manner you expect. This is one of the reasons that you miss opportunities. Now, are you going to open the door?"

Without further prodding, I touch the door, and it opens for me. Although it's heavy, it seems to respond to my touch as if it knows that I'm the right one to open it. We gingerly step in as we both duck under the archway. Upon first entrance, the room seems dark and musty as if no one has been here for a long time. As I continue to look around, I see objects on the walls. They look like musical instruments and other cool items, but I have no clue what they are.

Wisdom smiles as she watches me look about the room in amazement. "You do know where we are, don't you?"

"I think so. Are these unclaimed objects and gifts my ancestors didn't take?" I ask.

"Yes, and the reason you don't recognize some of them is because they are very old, and you never learned about them in your music history courses," she answers.

I was never a fan of music from the pre-Renaissance era. It makes sense that I don't recognize these instruments.

"These instruments represent sounds not heard for quite some time. And, some of them are new, too, reserved for this era. Remember that things from the past and present of your line can all be accessed now," she reminds me.

"That does make sense."

I go over to the wall and run my fingers along an instrument that looks like a lute. Then, I notice other wind and string instruments, all categorized according to their instrument families. This place actually looks like a well-maintained musical instrument museum. The only difference is that I can tell that all of these instruments are in pristine condition, not yet been touched by anyone.

"What am I supposed to do with them?" I ask.

"Pick them up and receive them into you as part of your being," she instructs.

She picks out a flute-like instrument and hands it to me. As I take it from her, I know that I'm to receive it into my body. I hold it up to my belly, and it disappears inside of me. I can feel it, almost as if it's playing in me.

"Wow! That's really cool!" I say while looking at my stomach.

"When something becomes a part of you, you will feel how it operates and works within you. Now, begin picking up these other instruments and receive them, too."

I walk along each wall, picking up instruments from all four families: woodwinds, brass, percussion, and strings. As I touch them, many disappear right into me.

"All of these instruments represent the sounds and music that's been put within you. Yes, you have a lot of head knowledge about music because of your training, but now, you will begin to function more out of a new sound that God has given to you. What you've done in the last year is a start, but more is coming. Be ready for it!"

I feel like a child in a candy store! Seeing all of these instruments makes me think of all the cool ways that I can use them.

"Thank you for bringing me here and teaching me more about what I need to know," I offer to Wisdom. "I guess that I am supposed to stay in music. And to think that I almost gave it up!"

I think of a time in my marriage where I shoved my clarinet in the back corner of a room and said that I was going to quit music and never play again. Recognizing that this was an unhealthy vow, I own, repent, and renounce those words and actions right here before Wisdom.

"Well done!" Wisdom immediately responds. "When the focus goes off YHVH and onto circumstances, it's easy to give up. This is an integral part of your destiny scroll. As you give more of yourself in worship and walk more in what you've been called to do, more will open up for you. What you've started is only the beginning. Continue moving forward in what you know to do."

I turn to face Wisdom, momentarily looking into her eyes. All I want to do is embrace her. Sensing my thoughts, she wraps her arms around me while we stand. I listen to the worship resonating throughout the Kingdom Realms while we embrace.

## The Lesson in This

Although this might seem as if it were for me personally, a lesson is in it for everyone. We all have gifts and objects from our ancestral lines that have been untouched by those who came before us. I address that with Seneca and Alice in our first book, Accessing Your Spiritual Inheritance.

As you begin to look at what's been left by your ancestors—ministries, jobs, talents, abilities, personal characteristics, and more—you can reclaim them for you and your future generations. Although I don't know of any budding musicians in my current family line, others will come along who have the opportunity to receive some of these instruments. I left several in the room that I knew were meant for others on both sides of my family. This opened up the possibility for them to receive what YHVH has for them.

I have yet to understand many aspects of this encounter. As I continue to reengage with this experience, I'll learn more. You will face similar experiences as you begin to receive what's meant for you and your ancestral line.

## Chapter Resources

- Both Ian Clayton (Son of Thunder Ministries) along with Grant and Sam Mahoney (Moed Ministries) have teachings on your DNA.

- Buy the book, Accessing Your Spiritual Inheritance, by myself, Seneca Schurbon, and Alice Briggs. The overall point of the book is learning how to access what was left behind by your ancestors.

## Chapter 9

# CASTLE OF MY HEART

As I ascend a marble stairway into the Kingdom Realms, a door opens. Before me, I hear what sounds like a party. Looking to my right, I see a castle-like building with a gothic look to it. I see myself flying around it at breakneck speed. The atmosphere is misty and gray outside with not much else visible. I don't want to be here. Taking a step back, I wait to see what this is all about. For the moment, I'm alone, but I sense that I'm here for a reason. I hear a voice.

"This is what it's like when you're trying to do things in your own strength. You feel like you're going around in circles with no support," says the voice.

"What am I doing?"

"You're operating out of your own strength. No, not today but what you did then is affecting today. You do know when this was, correct?"

I knew this was the voice of my Father.

Hanging my head, I reply "Yes. This is how I've acted most of my life." I feel the weight of that truth sink on me as the darkness closes in.

"And, it took you some time to learn, didn't it?" Father speaks gently.

"I still feel like I'm learning. However, I had no idea it looked this dark," I reply.

I look up, cocking my head as recognition dawns on me. Staring at the castle, I understand where we are.

"That's the castle of my heart, isn't it?" I question.

"Yes, it was and is when you go back to that place. You see, when you do things in your own strength, it shuts everyone else off from you. You have to decide and choose to walk in My light so that you can be infused with My glory. From that place, you can see where to go," Father adds even more gently.

"I'm so sorry, Lord, that I shut You out. All I ever wanted was to do Your will and walk with You. I do know that I forced things."

"And that's what got you to this place," He replies tenderly.

I sit on the wall, still feeling alone, watching myself spin around the castle. I know Father is with me and that there's something that I need to do, but I don't know what it is.

"Shed light on it," says Father.

"How do I do that?"

Spin... spin... spin. I continue to watch myself, almost to the point of becoming dizzy.

"Breathe on it and speak the light and glory of God into your soul," He instructs.

I take a deep breath, knowing I'm releasing the breath of God from within my spirit. Slowly, I blow toward the castle. As I do this, my spirit grows bigger and bigger. Quickly, I see that my spirit is bigger than the castle. I see myself looking confused as I stop circling around the castle while looking about. As my spirit breathes, light begins to envelop the area, and the sun begins to shine, rising over a hill as I continue to breathe on the situation. Birds begin to sing, and I can see how beautiful the greenery is around the castle.

"Do you know when this was?" asks Father.

"It was during my marriage," I reply.

"Yes, and you looked at what was going on around you and tried to fix it out of your own strength. Yes, I know you looked to me. I heard you, but then, you tried to fix it yourself."

"How did I do that, Lord?"

"You didn't leave when you should have. You listened to his lies, and then, you said that you could handle it because you felt that if you behaved differently, he would change. It nearly destroyed you. You have now breathed new life into that situation. You know what to do next."

Father steps back, taking a place beside me.

Without further thought, I kneel down, my head now at the top of the castle, and I pray. "Father, I own being strong-willed, self-sufficient, stubborn, and overly religious about it. I put my beliefs before your desire, Father. So, I own all of it, renounce ties with it, and repent. I put it at the feet of Jesus and nail it to the cross where it is crucified. I then cover it with the blood of Jesus."

For a moment, I continue to sit, kneeling. As I do this, I sense the atmosphere around me begin to lighten up.

"I was in my heart, wasn't I?" I ask once I've finished.

"Yes, and you saw what baggage from the past can do. That's one of the reasons it's so important to quickly turn away from the sinful nature. Keep short accounts and forgive so that your heart doesn't become dark. You were shown this so that you can take care of what's holding you back. Like you've asked, I'm putting the coal to your lips and purifying you. I'm also burning the seedbed of the intents of your heart so that nothing can grow there that would hinder you. The baptism of fire has a way of exposing ugliness. Once you burn it all off, then my desires can grow. Now, water them," Father instructs.

As an act of faith, I turn inward and pour the glory of God into my heart where I can marinate in His love, purifying this dark spot caused by my sin.

"Thank you, Father. I want to be cleansed of the junk so that I can move into more intimacy with You. That was hard to look at and feel, but I know You feel it even more than I do."

"As you continue to learn, part of this journey is going to involve some tough things; stuff that's hard to face. However, when you're cleansed, more can be given to you. Now, look back at the castle."

I turn and see flowers growing everywhere: yellow daffodils, roses, lilacs, and all kinds of my favorite flowers. Hummers and other birds swoop down and play with each other. This picture differs greatly from what I saw before. I know this is part of taking control over my soul. I want to live out of my spirit, and I know this is part of how that's done.

"And, you're well on your way." Father answers my thoughts as He hugs me.

## The Lesson in This

We've all been through tough places in our lives that we'd rather forget. I share this encounter so that you can see that what happens to us in our past can frame our future until we walk through a purification and healing process. In the beginning, I had no idea what I was looking at or even why I was there. However, as I spent time with Father, I began to sense and even see what was going on.

I stayed in my marriage because of religious teaching and counsel that told me that I couldn't leave. That caused a chain reaction inside me—body, soul, and spirit—that was not healthy. Although this encounter took place nearly sixteen years after my divorce, I obviously hadn't addressed some dark spots in my heart. I had to own my part in what went wrong so that the corrupt DNA could be replaced with the Father's DNA, which was done through repentance. I had to be judged in this area through the cross of Christ to remove the blemishes so that I could now begin to walk into my full inheritance as a son of God.

I will say that after this, I began to experience some of the same physical symptoms that came from emotional roots in my marriage. Anytime we deal with our junk, the accuser quickly comes knocking to see how serious we really are in addressing what holds us back. The difference between my responses now versus those sixteen years ago has vastly changed. First of all, I gave into the physical symptoms of illness during my marriage because I didn't know what else to do. Now, I can take those symptoms to be judged in the mobile court, the court of accusations, so that what harassed me then won't pester me any longer. If they continue to be pesky little creatures, they are in contempt of court. In our natural world, we know what happens when someone is held in contempt of court. They run into serious problems.

My encouragement for you in this is to continue the journey of learning to function in Him. When things come up from your past that need to be dealt with, take care of them quickly. Then, be prepared to deal with everything in the Kingdom Realms so that you truly have victory. What the accuser does should have no effect. I really like what Smith Wigglesworth used to do. A presence in his room sometimes woke him up in the middle of the night. Upon realizing it was the accuser, he looked at the enemy and stated, "Oh, it's you." Smith would then go back to sleep. What a way to disarm an enemy!

Where is the focus? Will it be on the Father or on the accuser? The more you focus on intimacy with Father, the quicker you'll see headway against what's holding you back.

**Chapter Practice and Resources**
- Grant and Sam Mahoney's teaching, "DNA Reconciliation School—Bloodlines," will help you clean out the junk.
- Ian Clayton's teachings, "The DNA of God" and "Inheriting Your Birthright," along with a teaching set titled "Keys to Living in Victory" will also provide you with further insight.
- Go before Jesus and ask Him to show you places in your heart that have been seared by choices you've made that have hurt you. This might include conscious as well as unconscious choices. The unconscious choices are often those that have been brought into you through your generational line. Since your DNA carries the memory of your lineage, stuff that you don't even know about might trigger certain behaviors in you, such as a propensity for alcoholism.

## Chapter 10

# THE MOBILE COURT

Ascending into His presence, I ponder on how to learn to function in Kingdom finances. As with many other times of entering the Kingdom Realms, I stand in an area of light but don't see much around me. I know this is the very entrance, that space that divides the two realms—my reality (the earthly realm) from that of my Father's realm.

"Let's go to court!" Jesus announces as He appears out of nowhere.

I know this is a response to my question about finances.

"Let's do it!" I exclaim as I notice my physical body start to shoot what looks like sparks out of my stomach area. I feel around and can't figure out where they are coming from.

Laughing, Jesus responds "As you mature and walk in my ways, your body will do some strange things. That was a bit of glory on you that you actually saw with your physical eyes."

"I'll take it! It surprised me since I wasn't expecting it," I offer.

"Now, to the courtroom!" Jesus responds gleefully.

Grabbing my hand, He leads me to a place on the left. I can't see where we're headed, but the next thing I know, we're standing in front of a door that looks like a courtroom entrance. He motions for me to open it. As I do and as I step in, I see the judge's bench. At first, because the room seems dimly lit, I can't see anyone. Then, as my eyes adjust and the light comes up in the room, I see Papa sitting at the bench with Jesus now to His right. I see the accuser to the left as a dark blob with angry eyes wringing his hands. Behind me, people begin to file in. I see my grandparents and others that I know are from my family line walk in. They seem to know that this is going to be some doozy of a court case.

I take my position in the defendant's chair on the left. After a time, the courtroom is full. Others are in the room that I don't recognize. I know they are from the cloud of witnesses and are here on my behalf.

A gavel comes down with a crashing sound that resonates throughout the courtroom. Everything grows very quiet as Papa rumbles, "Order in the court!"

Looking in my direction, then to the accuser, YHVH asks, "What are the charges?"

Eager to respond, he answers, "Greed of family finances, wanting, and hoarding it all!" He gives a sinister laugh, somehow thinking that this will intimidate me, then continues, "Poverty mentality, lack of financial self-control, and gluttony."

# The Mobile Court

The word "gluttony" flits through my mind. I wonder what that has to do with finances.

"How do you plead?" YHVH asks me.

"Guilty on all charges," I respond as I stand to accept the charges.

For a moment, I wait.

Then, looking at Jesus, I continue, "I own all of these. I repent and renounce each and every one on behalf of myself and my entire ancestral line, both parents. I nail them all to the cross where they are crucified." I then walk them through the cross to the other side where they are covered by the blood of Jesus.

Standing still, I allow the blood of Jesus to flow over and through me. Closing my eyes, I envision His blood washing away this sin. The courtroom is quiet, and I can tell the accuser is suddenly gone.

The noise of a door opening breaks the quiet. I turn as Melchizedek enters the courtroom.

The gavel cracks down again, and the voice of YHVH thunders, "You're forgiven. The slate has been wiped clean, and your accuser has left the room."

He scribbles something on a piece of parchment paper, then motions for me to come forward.

"This scroll is the decree freeing you from that bondage. Now, take it to the court of scribes to be recorded. Then, make sure that Melchizedek receives a copy. You keep one as well," Father instructs.

Jesus walks up next to me. As we leave the courtroom, I understand that the scroll is a declaration of my freedom from what held me back. I also know it's a release of finances into me as well as into my generational line.

The moment we step out of the courtroom, I'm in the court of the scribes. I hand an angel, who looks like a man not much taller than me, the scroll. He disappears for a moment, then comes back with copies of the original scroll. He hands them both to me, and I turn to leave.

Outside the courtroom once again, I'm aware that Jesus is with me, and we're instantly someplace else—the Treasury Room where Melchizedek greats us. I hand Him one scroll. He gladly accepts it, filing it with others around a corner. I take the other copy, and we leave.

"Remember to keep this in your heart." Jesus says, pointing to the last scroll. "You might have to use it again."

Understanding what He means by that, I hold the scroll up to my body, and it disappears inside of me.

## The Lesson in This

This encounter came out of many discussions with Father about how to deal with finances. In this world, we often struggle to understand the processes of making the needed adjustments in how we should "see" things, according to YHVH.

Let me preface any further discussion about the courts with this 411—many teachings about the courts of heaven abound. In a natural court of law on this earth, you can never take someone to court to be judged if they aren't there with you unless you have power of attorney for that person and they cannot speak for themselves, for example, if they are in a coma or something similarly drastic.

Why would we even think that we could go to the heavenly courts on behalf of another person? That is witchcraft because you're manipulating the will of someone else. Please consider this when

## The Mobile Court

listening to various teachings. Even so, you can go to court with people and stand beside them. You can pray and intercede for YHVH's will and desire for that person (salvation, blessings, etc.). For anything concerning a judgment, they must know beforehand and agree to go to court with you. You cannot do it without their knowledge. If someone has wronged you, you can only go to court on your behalf by accepting any charges they might have brought against you. This is what it means to agree quickly with the adversary (Matthew. 5:25). Doing it this way allows the Father to work with that other person. Dragging them into the heavenly courts without their permission and/or knowledge will not fare well for you.

With that understanding, I frequently find myself in court, dealing with my own issues as I did in this situation. We take care of ourselves and the junk that we carry first before we focus on others. People will wrong you and accuse you of the stupidest things. Fine, go ahead and accept the accusations immediately. This instantly disarms the accuser, freeing you. I learned this the hard way with a challenging situation. Three years later, I finally woke up and realized that once I owned what I was being accused of, it no longer bothered me. I had peace once I took it to court so that when I was confronted again, I didn't have the same reactions. In the natural, the situation took time to change. My attitude had to change first.

We take care of situations for ourselves and of those that surround our personal lives in the "mobile court" or the "court of accusation" in the Kingdom Realms. After this encounter, I began to experience financial freedom for the first time in many years. It required owning, repenting, and renouncing sin on my own behalf and for my ancestral line since I carry their DNA. I also carry the memory of everything they've done in my DNA. Therefore, repenting on my ancestor's behalf frees not only me but those in my family.

In some instances, you see immediate results, but other cases take more time. Build your faith to believe what you took care of is brought to earth and manifested around you. I had to change some paradigms concerning money and finances in general. Paradigms take time and effort to adjust. As such, don't expect a quick fix when you go to the mobile court.

**Chapter Practice and Resources**
- Ian Clayton has a great teaching series, "Kingdom Government," on his website where you'll see the teaching series for Kingdom Government I, II, and III.
- Grant and Sam Mahoney have a teaching set titled "Judicially Mandated—Heaven's Courts." It's on their shop page at the Moed Ministries website.
- Mike Parsons has two teachings on the courts from the "Deep Calls to Deep" conference with the NW Ekklesia in 2015. In session 8, he talks about the courts of heaven. He has another teaching from this same conference titled "The Court of Accusation." This is the court that I was in for the financial matter I discuss above. Go to YouTube, type in "Mike Parsons Deep Calls to Deep," and you'll find both teachings.
- For your own practice, when you are dealing with various situations in your life, focus on a picture of a courtroom in your mind. Then, if you need help, follow the steps in Mike Parson's "Court of Accusations" teaching as a starting point. You might see different things than what he describes. That's okay.

- If you find yourself in a court where you are asked to trade something for the verdict, get out! If you're unsure of where you are, look to see that Jesus and the Father are with you. Jesus will only ask you to own, repent, and renounce sin, nothing else. The only way you'll end up somewhere that you're not supposed to be is when your motive and agenda doesn't line up with the heart of YHVH. Most often, this happens when we take others to court without their knowledge and/or permission. Don't do it.

## Chapter 11

# THE MUSICAL INSTRUMENT ROOM

"Jesus, I understand that heaven has a musical instrument room. May I go there?" I ask, looking into the Kingdom Realms while ascending into His presence.

Jesus meets me as I walk down the path toward the bench by the river. I hug Him, and we sit, watching the rainbow fish swim. I'm happy to be in His presence, so I let the question go. As I sit close to Him, I feel the frequency of His love soak through me. I understand what it's like to marinate in His love and allow what He has to infuse into me, much like a sun tan. However, in this case, it's a "Son tan." At that thought, I giggle.

Jesus chuckles and puts His arm around me. Leaning my head on His chest, I feel His vibration even stronger. I then see a frequency that looks like a green light string weave around in the air between the two of us before it dances into me as though it's moving to its own music. Soon after, a blue light string does a similar dance, backwards, then forwards. Finally, it goes up, then down. After this dance, it, too, enters my heart just as the green strand did.

This pattern of "Son tanning" continues on for many days. Eventually, I begin to feel a frequency change in my physical heart. I notice that we are standing outside a very tall and ornate-looking door, similar to those from the Renaissance era, the entrance doors to castles. However, this door seems to tell the story of heaven through pictures. I see angels and some scenes that I can't quite make out yet. At this moment, I realize that when I'm reading scrolls, they can also be pictures—much like many ancient languages are pictorial.

"Good observation," Jesus says, responding to my thoughts. "It's too easy for your natural mind to lock into what you already know. When you think that you can only see writing in the English language, you are putting expectations on how you think things should look."

"I understand that now," I answer, remembering previous experiences of when I saw movies on the scrolls in the beaver's den. When I opened one of the scrolls, a picture turned into a movie.

"Look more closely at this door," Jesus instructs while pointing to a specific spot.

My eyes zero in on the scene—a creature that looks like an angel with stones across his body, wearing the nine-stone breastplate. The creature looks like a giant set of pipe organs with other instruments built into it—all instruments at the same time. I know this is Lucifer before he fell. Gazing at his majestic beauty, I understand a bit more of who he was created to be.

## The Musical Instrument Room

My eyes then span to the left for the next scene—Lucifer is being thrown out of heaven, stripped of all that beauty. I am sad that he would give up so much just to be noticed and have control.

Not wanting to linger too long on that image, my gaze moves a bit more to the left where I see all of the musical instruments from Lucifer's body all neatly laid out in rows according to instrument families—woodwinds, brass, strings, other pipes, and all types of percussion instruments, some of these conventional and others I've never seen before.

"These are waiting for the sons of God to pick them up and use them. As you know, they create the frequency of heaven when used as they are meant to be used."

I continue to look carefully over more pictures as Jesus talks.

"Now, it's time to open the door," He instructs.

I look but don't see a door knob or a place to put a key.

"Sing!" Jesus gleefully states.

Without questioning why, I begin to sing in the spirit, which turns to worship, where I'm twirling, singing, and dancing. I then notice that the instruments on the door interact with my worship. Colors swirl around me. Angels come to join as we all stand before this door, literally engaging with the door. Out of the colors come shapes. Our entire environment responds to our worship.

After some time, the door begins to slowly open. I sense our worship permits us to enter.

"You are correct in that thought," Jesus replies. "True worship opens the door to more. What's in this room is reserved for true worshipers. To open the door, you must do so with a pure heart. When you've hit the needed frequency, the door opens. By marinating in My frequency over the last several days, you have gone to a new level of intimacy with Me."

I look at Jesus and feel His love flow into and through me. He reaches over, pulling me into Him. As He does this, I feel a stronger and deeper love than before. We embrace in this place, and as we do, I feel more alive than before. I sense that as I cultivate this intimacy, I will see more.

"Yes, my dear one," Jesus responds in a loving tone, looking me right in the eyes. "Intimacy with Me and My Father is what unlocks the contents to this room."

"Thank you, Jesus, for showing me how to enter and helping me understand what's needed for me to engage here."

"You've been learning and hearing that everything comes through a higher level of intimacy. As you develop that intimacy, more authority is opened up before you. At this time, you're also seeing those who want this for personal gain. However, this will only work to a certain level because the lack of maturity might cause backlash. If people learn from their mistakes, they can then move to the next level of authority. I give people grace up to a certain point, just like parents do with a two-year old. As a twenty-year old, parents have an expectation that the son knows what to do and how to do it. He has more responsibility as he matures. Never forget that intimacy comes first and everything else flows from that intimacy, much like the door to this room full of instruments has opened to you as you engage through intimacy with Me," Jesus says softly while looking deeply into my eyes.

I look back as I listen to music coming from the instrument room. As I stare from His perspective, I know that all I have to do is step into them for more revelation to the past, present, and future. I know that He wants to show me more here.

We turn around and look into this magnificent room full of musical instruments. As on the door, they are laid out according to

## The Musical Instrument Room

families. Although the room has no lightbulbs or lamps, the gold walls provide all the needed light. I don't know how to explain what that looks like, but I do know that the gold illuminates the room brightly enough to see everything within it.

Walking up to a group of instruments, I ask, "Why are all of these here?"

"They have been left behind or stolen from those who were to use them. The sons of God are to use these instruments to bring My frequency into the earth's realms. The instruments wait for the sons who will learn what to do with them," Jesus answers.

"Is there anything I need to reclaim from my generational line—either my mother's or my father's side?" I ask.

"Follow Me," Jesus responds as He motions me to a pathway on the right.

We pass tables and shelves full of instruments, many labeled with family names. Some have many instruments, and others have only a few. We continue to walk down a hallway or a room like a path between shelves and tables of instruments.

Finally, we stop at two sections right across from each other. I see my father's family name on the left and my mother's on the right. On my mother's shelf, I see very few instruments. But, on my father's side, I see a beautiful drum kit. I look at it for a moment, wondering.

"Remember the eras when they wouldn't allow certain instruments and rhythms into the house of God?" Jesus questions.

"Yes," I answer, thinking back to my own church as a child and remembering how drums were often banished in worship.

I stare at the drum kit and hear another set of footprints coming down the path. I turn to look and see a very tall bearded man wearing a plaid shirt. As in previous encounters, I know this to be Father, my Papa and my Friend. He smiles as He approaches and then without warning, He scoops me up into His arms and lifts me up to a very tall shelf on my mother's side. On the shelf, sitting way toward the back, is a single instrument.

"Why don't you reach back and grab it?" Papa instructs.

I stretch out my body and reach into the shelf, pulling out this funny-looking instrument, shaped much like the serpent instrument from the Renaissance era. I'm a bit puzzled as I turn over the instrument, examining it.

"That's how long ago this was left here," Jesus says, while looking over my shoulder.

"The members of your family, on your mother's side, were master craftsmen at one time. Some of them even made musical instruments. The serpent was very popular back in the day as you know from studying music history," Papa says, winking at me.

"Take it and blow into it!" Jesus says excitedly.

Holding the instrument up to my lips, I cover the appropriate finger holes and blow with all my might.

A sound begins to reverberate around the room, and I hear other instruments respond to it. I listen for a bit at the sounds coming back at me, like a full symphony.

"Now, take the instrument and put it into you," instructs Papa.

He points to my belly where I immediately take the instrument and push it in with complete ease. I don't feel any different. But I do know the instrument went in.

Papa then puts me down so that I can see the drum kit again.

"This is a special drum kit," Jesus says with a twinkle in His eye. "During your generation, drums, along with all those rock-and-roll beats, were banned from many churches. You have a brother who wanted to be a rock musician. These drums are the redemption of

# The Musical Instrument Room

what was taken from him because of the harmful and judgmental words spoken against his passion, a passion that I put within him."

I look at this beautiful drum kit, seeing it sparkle with gems of every kind.

"This instrument is for your own generational line and for those who want to pick back up what was stolen from them," Papa adds.

"Let all the frequencies, rhythms, and melodies be reclaimed!" I shout, holding up the serpent.

The room erupts in sound as I declare that all that's been stolen be returned to my family. I even pronounce this over myself. I know that my choice of a musical career was frowned upon at one point in the church my family attended.

Once again, I look at the shelf on my father's side and see a bunch of percussion instruments. I know that these are for me, and I gladly start to gather them up. As I do, they soak into me. Many are familiar and others I've never seen before.

"Once you're done, go to the Sea of Glass and trade them for more," Jesus instructs.

With glee, I start running down the pathway back the way we came, making music all the way. Jesus and Papa follow, both giggling at my excitement.

The next thing I realize, I'm on the Sea of Glass. I immediately take all of the instruments out of me and lay them neatly before the throne. Bowing before the throne, I offer them to Father.

"Father, I bring everything I've gathered that's been lost or stolen from my family that I've now retrieved. I put them before you on behalf of myself and my family. I trade them for more of You in all of our lives."

73

I watch as the instruments transform into more beautiful versions. I understand, with no words spoken, that I'm to pick them back up and put them in me once again.

## The Lesson in This

This encounter was extra special for me. Why is it here? Again, you see that Jesus and Father care about me and my generational line. Let's say that your family line is into starting and running businesses. I wouldn't be surprised if you eventually were invited to a place to gain more strategy for those businesses and even see things people before you left untouched. The point here is that what you do, the Father cares about. Those giftings are put within you so that you can fulfill here on earth what you're called to do. Even if things are left untouched by your ancestors, you still have the opportunity to recover those loses. Again, this is presented in more detail in the book, Accessing Your Spiritual Inheritance.

In this encounter, Father and Jesus show me what's meant for me. I understand what's being spoken to me although this isn't the case in every situation. However, the language and situations that you do understand will be used so that you can grasp what's presented before you. If you don't know what's happening, you need to search out the answer.

Here's an example from my own life. Math has never made sense to me, so I'm not a fan. When I began researching information on frequencies, I was faced with some mathematics. In encounters and experiences with Jesus and Father, they use simple pictorials to "show" me math. They are great teachers and know exactly how to help me understand difficult concepts. I'm still a long way from understanding many of these concepts, but the more I engage and

# The Musical Instrument Room

put myself in situations where I might be a bit uncomfortable, the more they make sense to me.

My encouragement to you through this experience is to ask about what's in your ancestral line. If you see similar careers or passions that continue through your lineage, you probably need to pay attention to those. As noted before, be sure to write down what you hear, see, sense, and feel so that you can go back and ask more questions as you remember. If you don't write down your questions, chances are you won't remember what to ask later when you reengage.

**Chapter Practice**

- At some point, ask to be taken to the Strategy Room in heaven. I've actually visited this room several times and have gained much strategy on how to run my business, Healing Frequencies Music. I share that experience in Praying Medic's book, Traveling in the Spirit Made Simple.
- As you begin to clean out your DNA, you will see and be given gifts and objects that were meant for your entire ancestral line that were either left behind or that were untouched. Some of those items might be for you and others might be for family members. As you receive them back in the spirit realm, they can be released by faith into the natural realm. I have not yet seen many of the items that I've received manifest yet in the earthly realm. Don't be surprised if this happens for you. If anything, you'll first see attitude changes and freedom in your family members.

- Terms:
    - Scrolls: Scrolls are blueprints or mandates that are meant to be carried out by the sons of God, you and me.
    - Trading: Trading in the Kingdom Realms is taking anything you receive and giving it to the Father for more of Him. Everything we do is a form of trading. Basically, we give something to get something else.

## Chapter 12

# ORCHESTRATION OF DNA

"Father, I come into Your presence seeking more direction on questions I have about DNA," I ask as I go up a marble stairway into the Kingdom Realms.

Jesus meets me at the door, opening it for me. We hug, and He motions for me to walk in front of Him. I immediately see a field of green grass all perfectly manicured with no imperfections of any kind. The grass appears to greet me as I interact with it.

"Follow me," Jesus instructs as we walk through the middle of the grass into what looks like a group of clouds that reach all the way to the ground.

We walk side by side, not saying anything. I enjoy being in His presence, soaking up the energy and strength that emanates from

Him. I sense that my cellular structure is memorizing what's going into me.

"That's exactly what's happening," Jesus responds to my thoughts. "As you pray during communion, that record goes into you. As you continue to focus on communion, this process will make more and more sense to you."

I smile as we continue to walk, not feeling the need to say anything. I know that I'll learn what I'm supposed to as I spend time with Him. I watch the grass turn as it greets us, then immediately spring back into perfect position once we walk over it.

"I'm trying to take control over my soul and flesh, but I'm still not very good at focusing on heaven when I'm trying to multi-task. In reality, if I could, I would love to figure out how to be in two places at once," I ponder.

"You will learn soon enough as you continue to practice. Your soul has had a long time to bully your spirit. When your spirit stands up and takes its rightful place, you have to continually remind your soul who's in charge," Jesus replies.

He stops and points ahead of us. "Now, we're here."

In front of me, I see a cloud, and the surrounding atmosphere instantly becomes like a gray and rainy day, only there's no rain or humidity; it's perfectly dry. We step into the cloud when I notice a white horse approaching. As it nears, I see that it doesn't have a saddle. Jesus and I stand together, watching. It stops directly in front of us and looks at me. I can hear its thoughts, beckoning me to mount it. I turn toward Jesus with a look of confusion. He motions for me to get on. With no saddle or reins, I wonder how I can accomplish this since the horse is so tall. Somehow, I'm able to mount the horse just by thinking about it. Jesus then hops on behind me.

## Orchestration of DNA

Immediately, the horse takes off and heads deeper into the cloud. It's growing darker and darker. Soon, I see objects whizzing by so fast that I can't tell what it is. We continue riding without any conversation. Somehow, I know not to ask where we are yet. At that thought, Jesus smiles.

We continue, and I start to see circular items buzzing and spinning but not moving as fast as the other flying objects. It's dark, yet it's not. Light is coming from somewhere, but I can't tell from where. I then start seeing other shapes: triangles, squares, octagons, and other shapes, float by. Each seems to have a direction and place to be, none hitting or touching the others despite the fact that they are all around us by now. So much sparkle is in the air that I feel as if I'm under a cloud of glitter falling from above. The odd part is that nothing touches us.

"We are in a cell," Jesus finally speaks. "What you are seeing represents all the parts and pieces that are building blocks of creation. As you see, everything has color, movement, and a direction. You can actually see the vibrations of some items. They all work together in harmony, just as an orchestra is full of different musicians and parts that make up the whole when the conductor starts a piece of music. As in music, when someone makes a wrong entrance or a wrong note, it's recorded until a recording engineer removes the error."

Jesus looks at me as I let this soak in for a bit.

He continues, "My blood is like what that engineer does You've watched it during recording and mixing processes. The files are opened for editing. The engineer can take out a single wrong note after the musician records a new correct note, replacing the bad note with the new one. In the final recording, you'll never hear the wrong note because it's been replaced with the correct one. When I cleanse your DNA, it's like editing the mistake or corruption out and replacing it with my DNA, which is not corrupt. What you're looking at is a cell that functions according to my DNA."

I look and see this symphony of movement and view it from that perspective. Although so many bits and pieces are flying all around, I can tell they all have a rhythm, each slightly different. They all work harmoniously together. I ponder the rhythm.

"That's part of it," Jesus responds to my thoughts. "Rhythm is the backbone that holds it all together. Frequency is a rhythm as well as a pitch. Together, we have rhythm, pitch, and space or rests. Space in time is what musicians call rests. The rests are as important as the actual rhythm and pitches, which you've heard taught by conducting instructors."

I think back to conducting classes. The preparatory beat given before the first note of music is even sounded is important because it, too, has motion. Without it, the musicians wouldn't know when to start the music.

"Everything in heaven is mirrored on earth," Jesus continues while pointing to a wriggling cell floating by. "You are used to seeing it in music. My blueprint of DNA is also in music. As you continue to study, you'll see it in music theory. This will help you understand how DNA functions."

We turn and continue to watch this symphony of movement around us as I ponder His words. The cool part is that I understand a bit better how taking communion is a form of replacing corrupt DNA, just as a recording engineer takes a piece of music with mistakes and edits out wrong notes. How awesome of Jesus to use an example of something I've recently witnessed while working in the recording studio.

Jesus winks at me, pulling me closer as we continue to watch the DNA dance before us.

## The Lesson in This

What I find interesting with this encounter is how Jesus used an example from something I'd just witnessed in a recording studio in addition to a documentary I'd seen on DNA.

As you continue on your own journey into intimacy, you'll gain insight into what's on your life's blueprint or scroll of testimony. We are each called to "be" a piece of a puzzle. When brought together with others, we create the perfect picture of a complete puzzle. I use this analogy here because puzzles have many pieces. When puzzle pieces are missing, you can't see the whole picture. Nothing can be done until all the pieces are put into place. My puzzle involves music and frequencies; others have pieces as well. Your puzzle might be something totally different.

This encounter helped me understand the importance of taking communion and what it actually does more in depth. As we take communion by faith, we are actually replacing humanistic DNA with that of the Father. I have noticed a physical improvement in my body after taking communion several times a day for over two years.

If you want to see changes in your physical body, start taking communion. You likely won't see immediate results. However, as you continue taking communion, you'll eventually see changes. The key here is to not give up!

## Chapter Practice and Resources

- Take communion daily—several times—both physically and in the spirit. Taking communion in the spirit simply means putting your body on the altar to present yourself to God in your imagination and then visualizing yourself taking communion. I can't stress enough how important taking communion is! Ian Clayton has a teaching set entitled "Realms of the Kingdom" that includes an MP3 on communion.
- Take time daily to repent by going through your bloodlines and cleansing all of the DNA (memories, actions, thoughts, habits, and so forth) of those who went before you. If you make this part of your daily devotionals, you can also address any matters that creep up in your daily life.

## Chapter 13

# DIVIDING SOUL AND SPIRIT

I'm standing in a clearing in a forest, looking up at the sky, watching clouds dance to the music in heaven. Everything reacts to the worship, and I love to watch how it all responds.

After a moment, I sense Wisdom next to me. Together, we enjoy the activity in the atmosphere around us. I think of teachings about getting to know Wisdom.

"That is why you're here and why I'm with you. The Spirit of Understanding will help you retain that information," she answers my thoughts.

"In listening to a teaching about how the Queen of Sheba listened to Solomon answer all her hard questions. How did Solomon instantly have the knowledge and then understand what he was saying? That's different than having a word of knowledge," I question.

"Yes, with a word of knowledge, you don't often have understanding. You might have a word for someone but have no clue as to what it means. I think you use the word 'clueless' for that," she says, winking at me.

"Did Solomon instantly have wisdom, knowledge, and understanding of something?" I ask.

"Yes, because he was with the Father and understood how to function in the Kingdom Realms."

"Wow! I can see why people would really like that!"

"Remember, the motive is always known. If the motive is incorrect and people are lazy or want it for selfish gain, it won't do them any good. Also, remember that for those constant requests 'I must have . . . .' When they get what they ask for but their character doesn't match, it will destroy them. You saw that in your own marriage and even wrote about it in your book. When people's motives are not pure, too much of a good thing can have a very devastating effect. Todd kept wanting to be put in positions of authority as a preacher along with being well-respected. The problem is that it was for his own gain, like buying himself a place in the Kingdom. Ask yourself this question, 'Do you want something because you're trying to gain a position in the earthly realm, or are you trying to build relationship with YHVH and then out of that relationship, you're given responsibility?'"

"I think I'd rather have the second choice since relationship is most important. When you understand true character, you know what to expect," I add.

"That's why it's important to spend time with the seven Spirits of God, learn our character, and then see how we operate. It's like that phrase, 'monkey see—monkey do.' When you see us 'do,' then you can, too," she answers.

For a moment, we continue to watch the clouds dance. I see a couple of shooting stars even though it's completely light out.

After some time, I finally speak. "I do want to be with you and learn all that I'm supposed to. I'm still wrapping my mind around that proverbial paradigm shift so that I can gain wisdom and understanding in how to totally function from the Kingdom Realm and then bring that supply into the earth realm."

"That's why you're training with me and spending time in our presence so that you can learn and then do what's on your testimony scroll," Wisdom answers. "For example, look at these clouds. You've noticed they appear to dance and move to the music. How do they do that?"

"I guess that it has something to do with frequency and vibration," I offer.

"It's much more than that. Remember how the Word says that everything is groaning for the sons of God to take their place?" she asks.

"Yes."

"Everything went out of alignment from the original blueprint at the fall. The vibrational frequency was changed, but through worship and the sons of God walking out what's in their scrolls, creation is coming back into its intended frequency. These clouds are now vibrating at their intended frequency because one of the sons of God has spoken what God intended over them. They basically reframed and restructured their vibration by the spoken word," she instructs.

We continue to watch the clouds as Wisdom hugs me. I snuggle in closer and ponder how good it is to have her as a mother figure. Sounds of the song "I AM" waft from the stereo, and I can see the frequencies in my room intermingle with those in heaven. I wonder if this is really what it's like, bringing heaven to earth. Even though I wasn't aware of what was going on when I recorded the music at the time, was my spirit now responding to what I'm conscious of hearing?

"Your spirit remembers everything," Wisdom replies to my thoughts. "Remember that your spirit was with God in the beginning. You lack memory only because the soul has taken over, essentially shutting off the spirit memory. Until a person allows the spirit to control the soul, it's difficult for that memory to be prominent."

My mind immediately thinks of how the soul sits between the body and spirt. When it's in control, energy doesn't naturally flow from the heart to the body. I then picture how that looks—no straight lines!

Wisdom chuckles and adds, "That would be one way to explain it. Gaining control of the soul is all about letting the spirit stand up, and the soul bowing to the dictates of the spirit as you've heard taught. It's not functioning from the center but from some place along the line. So, in a sense, you're only half functioning because there isn't a connection from the heart to the body, flowing from the gateway of first love, to the spirit, then to the soul, and lastly, to the body. When function starts at the soul, the first two stages are totally left out. No wonder people struggle!"

She turns to look at me, her blonde hair glowing under the light. Her face is fresh and "living." Her eyes light up like gems. I'm not even sure what color they are because they seem to change. She looks lovingly into me. It's almost as if I can see thought frequencies coming out of her eyes.

## Dividing Soul and Spirit

"I want to understand more fully why it seems so difficult to divide the soul and spirit as described in Hebrews 4:12. I've listened to teachings on this subject for a very long time, practicing and by faith, driving a wedge between the two. However, I don't feel anything happen physically. Are they really divided, and if so, when?" I ask Wisdom.

"Why do you think your experiences will be like others? What do you see as the fruit in your own life based on your own experiences?" She responds with a more serious tone.

For a moment, I ponder and think about what this might look like. Over the last year, many things in my life have changed, most for the better.

She continues, "You are basing your expectations off other's description of their experiences. Yes, those are a good starting point, but you need to look at your own experiences. Dividing the soul and spirit is a daily exercise. You have over fifty years of baggage to unload."

I know what to do. I take a moment to repent for unhealthy expectations.

Wisdom offers, "You had a specific idea of what you thought would happen when the soul and spirit divide. However, if you look at the fruit in your life, you'll know how what you're practicing is working. Does that make sense?"

"I think I'm starting to get it!" I say, smiling as I continue to gaze into her eyes.

With that, we sit embracing on a bench that I didn't notice before. I soak up her affection, knowing this motherly hug is exactly what I need. Wow . . . the mother's embrace. I never really knew or understood how healing this simple act is for me.

As these thoughts cascade through my brain, Wisdom

responds by hugging me tighter.

## The Lesson in This

Expectations can easily get us into trouble. For me, this discussion with Wisdom was a lesson in learning that just because someone else has a specific experience on how to divide the soul from the spirit, doesn't mean that I will have exactly the same experience.

When God communicated with the Jews, He spoke to them using examples that they would understand. Jesus did the same when He told parables. It's no different with us today. Dividing the soul and spirit is all about allowing the spirit to control us instead of the soul. That means when emotions, physical issues in our lives, attitudes, and/or negative triggers creep in, our spirit should tell our soul how to respond. Normally, we tend to allow the soul to reign supreme. We've lived out of soul for so long that we seem to forget how to let the spirit be in charge. Again, it takes practice, patience, and perseverance to train the spirit to run the show. As I've learned, this doesn't happen overnight. In fact, you might take months before you even notice significant changes.

I share this story in my book, But Words Will Never Hurt Me, available on Amazon. My ex-husband went through a process of repentance. He spent a week secluded in our house before the Father. He eventually came upstairs and announced that he'd repented and dealt with the issues that plagued him. Now, it was my turn to do the same. The implication was that there would be no more behavior issues on his part, so anything negative in the future would come from me.

I hope that you can already see the problem with this. Yes, we can own, repent, and renounce sin, including our habits. However, the problem lies in unlearning the old ways and retraining ourselves to function in Christ. Habits take time to break. This includes thoughts, what comes flying out of our mouth, mindsets, attitudes, actions, and behaviors. Yes, God forgives immediately when we ask for it. However, we have the opportunity to walk it out, learning to be consistent. Habits happen when we don't have to think about what we are doing any longer. For most people, this takes sixty days or longer to intentionally and continually kick these habits in the butt.

What negatively triggers you? What is your first response when someone belittles you? How do you respond when you become angry? The answers to these and other questions can help determine which gateways of the soul need some work so that the soul and spirit can be accurately divided. When dividing the soul and spirit is well under way, our behavior will show the difference.

For the best results, I recommend that you obtain some teachings mentioned below on addressing the issues in your life that keep you in negative habits. Even if you've gone through counseling, you will still need to continue the process because the soul loves to be in charge, often feeling sorry for itself. As we allow the cleansing blood of Jesus to wash over us, we transform into His image.

## Chapter Practice and Resources

- Listen to Ian Clayton's teaching titled, "Dividing the Soul and Spirit," along with "Thoughts and Intents" and "Joints and Marrow." All three go together and should be listened to several times so that you can fully grasp the depths of the teaching.

# Postlude

Where do you go from here? As you develop intimacy with Father, you will have many opportunities to take care of those things in your life that keep you from moving forward. Let me give you an example by "telling" on myself.

I'm a type "A" personality, which lends itself to a show-off mentality. Maybe because this was a big issue through much of my life, I spot this tendency more easily in others. If I'm not careful to take my thoughts captive, this can become a negative trigger for me. As such, when I began this journey into intimacy, I found myself wanting to prove myself to others. I wanted to be important. I hoped prophetic people would give me the latest and greatest word. I relied on others to hear God for me. I went to conferences, expecting to receive a word of knowledge from the speaker(s) and was upset when I didn't. If a speaker didn't acknowledge me at some point in the conference, I felt "less than." Some of you reading this might know the drill and relate to me. I rarely said a word to anyone concerning my feelings and frustrations. However, the thoughts still ran through my mind. Conferences are meant to assist us on our journey, not to provide us with "daily bread" that we should receive through relationship with Father.

Father asked me one Christmas to seclude myself and to talk

to no one but Him for one month. Oh my! For me, that was asking a lot! No phone calls!? No checking the internet or Facebook to see what everyone was doing!? I'd already banned my TV to a shed, so what was I going to do for an entire month!? The thought of this was more than I could fathom at the time. I actually dreaded it when I started the journey with no idea of what to expect.

I had to like myself, be comfortable with who I was created to be, and then realize I am supposed to be in Him. After that initial month, over the next seven years, I began the process of rooting out old behaviors, thought patterns, intents, and motives that resulted from my need for approval, my need to be someone. I'm learning that Father promotes and when I step in and take over, I demote.

Before I go into the next section, understand that I speak from experience because I've done everything on this list. I'm maturing into who I'm supposed to be, too. Ask yourself the following questions as you go through your own cleansing process:

- Do you find yourself posting frustrations and struggles on social media? If so, what's your true motive for doing this?
- Do you run to others, asking for prayer every time you face a struggle in your job, family, finances, physical body, and so forth?
- Do you find yourself telling everyone all of the good things you've done? This often comes from a need to be noticed.
- Are your responses to others filled with accolades for yourself? An example of this might be when someone tells you what they see in the spirit and you immediately pipe up with your own story, basically "one upping" the other person's experience.
- Do you feel the need for confirmation for everything you see and do in the Kingdom?

- Do you expect others to serve and meet your needs? This could be financially, spiritually, emotionally, and even physically.
- Do you expect everything for free because Christians should share freely? This comes from a poverty mentality of thinking that other Christians should provide services, such as conferences, teaching materials, books, counseling, coaching, and any event or product for reduced prices or even for free.
- When you're with others, do you feel that they need to listen to your counsel?
- Do you follow through with what you say you'll do?
- Do you complete tasks or leave them unfinished?
- If Father asks you to do something, do you do it? Or, do you have excuses for not following through?
- Do you treat those you're around with respect? Examples of this might be:
  - Cleaning up after yourself,
  - Paying properly for services received, including tipping,
  - Calling out people openly on their sin,
  - Being unfriendly because you've taken offense to behaviors/harsh words/actions,
  - Feeling the need to explain yourself despite how others may receive it, and
  - The list could go on.

This is a journey. As I said earlier, character takes time to build. You will need to retrain your whole being to function out of God's character. Most of us have had many years of functioning from soul not spirit. This leads to poor character development. Retraining our mind, choices, will, emotions, imagination, reasoning, and conscience, our soul gates, and so forth involves stripping everything down to the bare bones so that it can be rebuilt in Father's character. This is similar to purchasing a 300-hundred-year-old house and renovating the entire structure from the foundation through the final decorative touches.

My goal is not to be harsh, it's to help you understand that when you make the decision to move into a deeper relationship with Father, your life will turn upside down. In the long run, that's a good thing because it will bring you into the fullness of who you are meant to be in Him. If you're ready, consider purchasing the teachings I've mentioned above along with those listed in the resources section at the end of this book. Don't just look for free material. If finances are an issue, have a discussion with Father on how to shift your paradigm in that area.

I will say that physical issues are the most difficult with which. Physical pain seems to drag us down the most. I've been there, so I know what it feels like. Even in the midst of that pain, we take our bodies to the Father and allow Him to infuse us with His DNA. This starts by faith, and even when we don't see results, we continue to stand. From faith, we begin to see results. Be thankful for even the smallest physical victories. Rejoicing for the tiny things helps build faith for the bigger ones. Learn to be thankful for what you do see instead of being frustrated with what you don't see. See the glass half full, not half empty.

# RESOURCES

### Ministries/Schools/Teachers

- Ian Clayton: www.sonofthunder.org. Click on the "resources" tab for teachings. In the left sidebar, you can click on a variety of choices, including books, conference sets, product bundles, CDs, and more. You can also put the name of the teaching in the search box.
- Mike Parson's: www.freedomtrust.org.uk. Sign up for the "Engaging God" series, an "at-your-own-pace" school.
- "The Nest" is a three-year school run by Ian Clayton with Grant and Samantha Mahoney. www.thefoundationnest.com.
- Grant and Samantha Mahoney of Moed Ministries teachings available at www.moed-ministries.com.
- Dr. Adonijah Ogbonnaya (Dr. O) has many of his teachings on his YouTube channel AACTEV8.
- NW Ekklesia (Northwest Ekklesia) is based on the west coast of the USA. They mentor through video conferencing in groups across the country set up for fall and spring sessions. Learn more at www.nwekklesia.com.
- Supernatural Lessons is the website I started when people began asking me about the changes in my life. I have several resources available to assist you on your own journey.

Accessing the Kingdom Realms

www.supernaturallessons.com.

**Healing/Counseling**

I put this group into its own category because the focus here is more on dealing with the junk you discover after you sit under the teachings of those in the first category.

- Moed Ministries is run by Grant and Sam Mahoney. Although they are listed above, they also provide counseling and mentoring sessions to people who need assistance. Their website is www.moed-ministries.com. Click on the "mentoring" tab to sign up for a mentor.
- Freedom Flowers is a flower essence company. Several "bouquet blends" are available to assist with emotional healing. Seneca makes her own essences from scratch (mother essence), praying into each essence. Seneca's website is www.freedom-flowers.com.
- Alice Briggs is with Emotional and Spiritual Healing. She's a Splankna practitioner with training in a variety of other inner healing techniques. She does in-person sessions or sessions over Skype. Alice was a major contributor to the book, Accessing Your Spiritual Inheritance. She's very insightful and hears from the Holy Spirit in how to assist you on your journey of wholeness. Her website is: www.emotionalandspiritualhealing.com.
- Healing Frequencies Music is my main website. I'd been listening to Ian Clayton teachings and doing all the activations for about six months, when a sudden shift seemed to hit me, and musical sounds started pouring out of me in a manner I'd never experienced before. www.healingfrequenciesmusic.com.

- Books:
    - Accessing Your Spiritual Inheritance by Alice Briggs, Del Hungerford, and Seneca Schurbon
    - The Order of Melchizedek and Realms of the Kingdom (Parts I and II) by Ian Clayton and
    - Freedom: Coming out from under the Curses of Freemasonry by Grant and Samantha Mahoney.

    All are available from Amazon.

For additional resources, visit my site at www.supernaturallessons.com.

# About the Author

Del has a firm grasp on the "art of practicing" that enables others to increase their capacity to encounter YHVH in new ways. She has applied her knowledge and training in classical music to her Supernatural Lessons classes. This provides a platform for others to experience and develop a deeper intimacy with YHVH via her intuitive music, which focuses on raising personal frequency to bring healing to body, mind, and soul.

Del has navigated through many seasons of life. Even during the rough times, she's learned to make lemonade out of lemons and sees the glass as half full. Although she's spent most of her career as a professional musician, she has taken many rabbit trails on other journeys. These life experiences have enabled her to cultivate the personal presence of YHVH in her life. From this place, she created spontaneous music, which then led her to assist others on their journeys to discover all that YHVH has for them.

Del gives others opportunities to practice engaging YHVH through her website, Supernatural Lessons, at www.supernaturallessons.com. Her music can be found at www.healingfrequenciesmusic.com.

Made in the USA
Middletown, DE
14 March 2018